JUST THOUGHTS

Words & Pictures
By Audrey Mac

Dedicated to my family
Always a beautiful source of
inspiration

WHERE I BELONG

I am always where I belong.

If not, why am I there?

I choose not to wander around
without a purpose or a care.

If I stray to an unknown land, a
mighty wind blows my hand

And with a light push and a turn of
my feet,

I am back where I belong.

FITTING IN

Am I ashamed of my own skin?

When did this begin?

The very thought that there is a norm,
a standard, a perfect hue - fills my
head with fiery fuel.

Who wrote these rules? Do you fit in?
Do I fit in? Does he fit in? Where does
it end?

I am here therefore I AM IN!

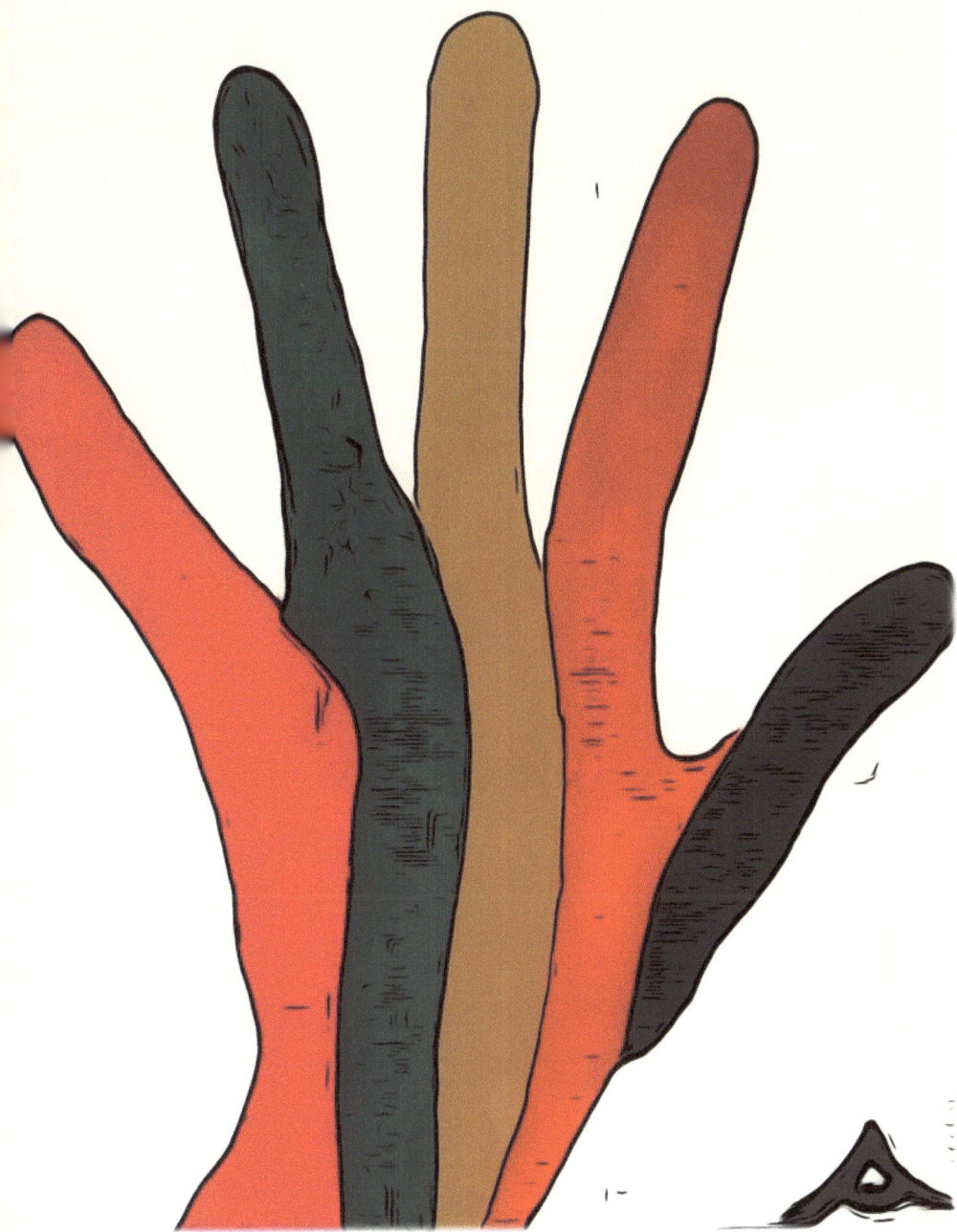

MY BACKPACK

My backpack is full.

Can't say that I put everything in it, but I left it wide open as I walked around.

Things got put in, things were taken out.

I laid it down and walked away and I can't remember what's inside.

Yet I still carry it - heavy and full.

I wonder what I would find if I clean it out.

EVERY MORNING

Each day is new.

Yesterday is a memory.

Time travel is not an option.

How much of today will you own, embrace and control? If only an hour, take it!

Do something you love each day.

Every morning is a clean slate to paint the picture you choose.

A MOMENT

Like the sound of music in a theatre or a concert hall, compared to the stereo in your home, the countryside is an acoustic dream.

Maybe it's the view, but the sound of silence with a light early morning chirping chorus amazed me.

A hummingbird!

In the city I would have never heard it. But sitting on a porch looking out at the Maine countryside . . . a five second buzzing sound as I looked up and saw it was astounding!

Even the sound of a car coming down the street is like a jet flying overhead at the local airshow. As a city girl I have never spent much time in the woods. I am so used to urban noises - music, tv, airplanes, cars, lawnmowers, dogs and of course, people. This feels like a new sound - a good sound.

Somehow, I have just become aware of all of the noise of my everyday life. An occasional timeout away from cell towers is cleansing. I call it *digital detox*.

For me, a break from the mind-numbing clutter where you feel like a hamster on an eternal wheel of activity. Enough - let's take a break!

EXPOSURE

Can I dream about something I cannot see? Could it ever be?

Things like that don't happen to me. What do you mean there's no limit for me?

This is me . . . this is it.

Show me, show me there is more. Help me kick open this locked door in my head with no windows.

I can't see it so, I can't be it. How do you become what you have never seen? Show me.

WORDS

Curling my hair getting ready to leave
. . .

Where did these words come from?

Why won't they stop?

Is this how creativity works?

Out of nowhere, at any time,
regardless of the space I'm in – gotta
go grab a pen!

As time ticks away, I know I've got to
stop.

Why won't they come when I have
nowhere to go?

WHAT DO YOU BELIEVE?

Do you believe you could be the richest or most famous person that every lived?

Do you believe that you might be the person that helps to cure a major disease?

Do you believe that your words could be spoken for many years to come through others you may never meet?

Do you believe that one of your ideas could transform millions of lives during your lifetime?

Do you believe that your life story could be talked about long after you are gone?

Do you believe that God placed you on Earth to be something someday that you could never have imagined?

"Mom, do you believe I could be that person?"

"Son, I believe in you, I believe in God and his plan for all of us."

"Ok mama. If you believe, I believe. Can I ask you a question?"

"Yes, son?"

"When you were my age, what did you believe?"

WE ARE ALL THE SAME

I breathe one moment at a time . . .
do you?

My skin can burn and my blood is red

. . . how about you?

My heart beats in my chest second by
second

. . . does yours?

My body needs rest to go on

. . . you feel it too?

My eyes see everything

. . . can yours?

My tongue speaks words I feel

. . . like you?

When my soul leaves this body and my life on Earth is over - guess what? This will happen to you too! We are ALL the same.

GRANDMA'S PRAYERS

Long before I was born,

    Grandma prayed for me.

As I entered into this world crying,

    Grandma prayed for me.

While I cooed, stumbled and grew,

    Grandma prayed for me.

Even when I pouted and
complained,

    Grandma prayed for me.

As I walked across the stage and left
for college,

    Grandma prayed for me.

When I traveled around the world trying to 'find myself',

Grandma prayed for me.

As I settled into the grind and started my own family,

Grandma prayed for me.

As she started her journey's end, at her bedside as I prayed for her,

Grandma *still* prayed for me.

CAN

How can you tell me what I can be?

Do you realize there's nobody,
NOBODY like me?

I don't care what you see, you don't
see it all.

Will you answer, when I get the
call?

To rise, to soar to places unseen

To do magical things for which you
can only dream

Don't box me, don't stop me or try
to categorize

Can you see what I see, if you don't
have these eyes?

THE NOISE

When I close my eyes, everything dies into a deep dark space of nothing.

Suddenly, a light appears and I am transported into a beautiful landscape of life, peace and joy.

Don't wake me up – I'd like to stay here awhile. Not forever, just a few more hours, I say with a smile.

Here, I am free. Nothing to do but sit, enjoy and take in the sights. No calling, texting, yelling, rambling, to do lists . . .

Why can't I find this place when I open my eyes?

ROAD BULLY

Ok, you've got a big truck.

So, what?

Do you own the road?

Should I be scared?

When you almost ran me off the road to
show how little you cared?

About my life, my safety, my well-being

Who are you hiding behind that wheel?
Encased in so much iron and steel.

Slow down, buddy. You're not that great.
You don't own this – why can't you wait?

AFTER HOURS

What goes on at school after hours? Do the books come alive? Do the chalkboards talk?

If I was here and the pet hamsters drew near would they talk about the day, and ask me if I was ok?

Would the desk start spinning around and throw everything on the ground? Why not? No one is here to hear the sound?

Would the pencils and the stencils join together with the kitchen utensils to create a food festival for the night critters to enjoy?

If so, who cleans the mess so I can safely sit at my desk the next day wishing I could be here again to see the nighttime play.

MY DAY

Saturday

> Rest day, play day, fun day, best day

Sunday

> Church day, family day, last day, pre-Monday

Monday

> Work day, start day, long day, "uggghh" day

Tuesday

> Another day, ok day, "get over it" day, planning day

Wednesday

> Busy day, hump day, yep day, short day

Thursday

Almost day, zone day, one more day, hurry day

Friday

Happy day, finally day, finish it day, "peace out" day

How's your day?

DO WORDS MATTER?

They

Love

Hurt

Cut

Grow

Drive

Crush

Build

Fill

Inspire

Fire

Breathe

Die

WHO CARES?

They don't like me?

Who cares

They think I'm weird?

Who cares

They laugh at me?

Who cares

They call me names?

Who cares

They leave me out?

Who cares

They say I won't make it?

Who cares

They try to stop me?

Who cares

Sounds easy . . .

Lord, help me so I won't care

ENOUGH

What's this word called enough?

As I look around, I've got so much stuff.

I don't think I can recall where I have put it all.

Do I need it? Do I want it? Do I even know it's there?

How on Earth did this happen? There's so much stuff everywhere.

I should find someone in need, who could appreciate a good deed.

Clearly, I have gone too far.

I have more than enough.

ROCKIN' THE HOUSE

I can't believe we're all so tired.

Just a while ago, everyone was wired.

Laughing, playing, singing, swaying

Partying like there's no tomorrow - no worries, no cares, no sadness or sorrow.

Walk in here now, you'd be startled to see

Everyone in bed, exhausted as can be

Traveling to dream space, looking
for a place to grace

As we snore as loud as we can,
underneath the ceiling fan

We sleep until we can party again
but we can't stop rocking the house

I CAN'T WIN ALONE

I need you to:

Guide me

Chastise me

Rule me

Grow me

Cheer me

Inspire me

Show me

Teach me

Hug me

Love me

Make me whole, help me win.

THE ANGEL

Sits above and watches me

Guides me with a little nudge

Drops random thoughts in my sights,
that I think are my own

Wakes me up without alarms

Helps me see what others won't

Shows me what I can really be

If only I would truly believe

Cares about how I get through this life

But can't control my choices

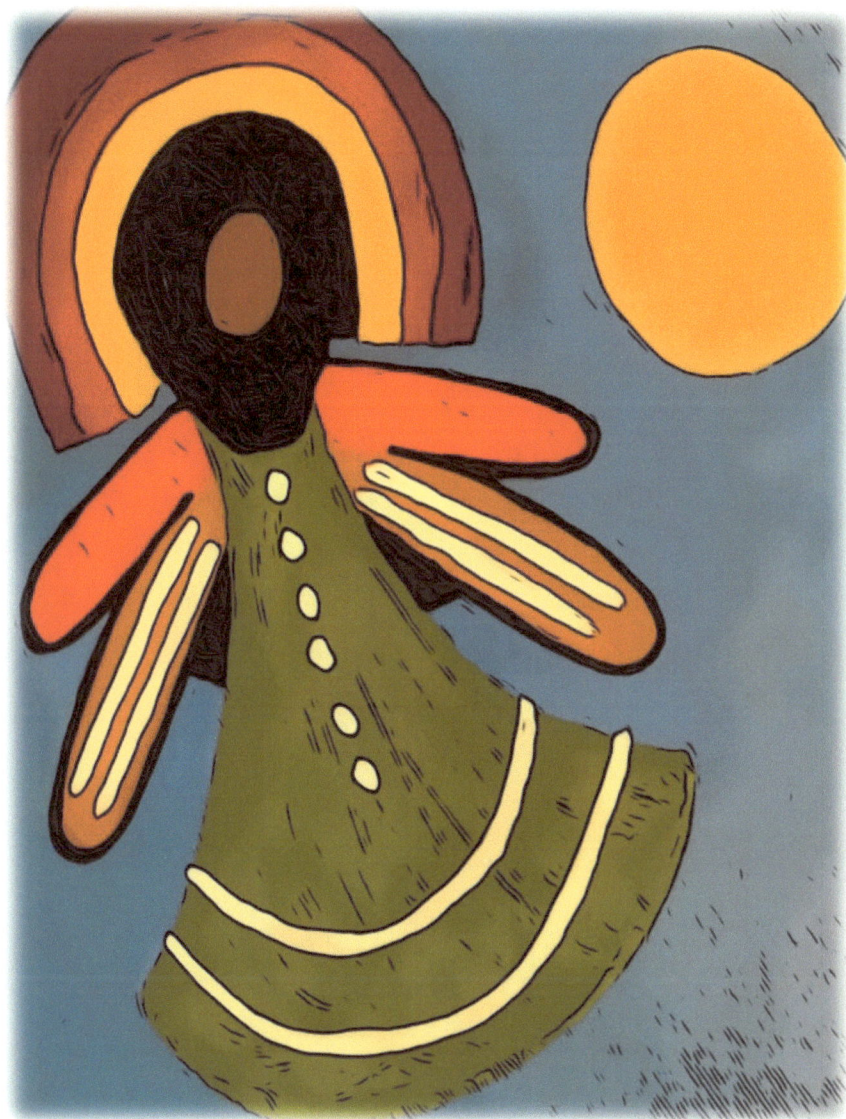

RUNNING

Hamster wheel spinning

Here I go, here I go running

Faster and faster in a little cage,

Going nowhere

Looking busy, almost spent

Jumping off to nap and rest

Waking up to get on again

Time to get back to work

Spinning, going nowhere

GROW

How big will I get?

No one knows, we'll see

My favorite shirt is short

These pants are too high

Toes are tight and my feet begin to
burn

Socks will stretch so there's no
worries there

Legs hanging off the bed

I like growing, but wonder when
will it stop.

SEEDS

Like a seed, I need things to grow and beautify.

Can you see my future with your mind's eye?

Fertilizer, water and the magnificent sun

Feeding me and kissing my skin, like a loved one taking care

Am I watered?

Am I fed?

Am I nurtured?

Am I led?

I need it all to thrive and grow like a seed waiting to come alive.

SOCIALLY

Yes, we spoke

I sent you a text

Don't you understand Generation
Next

We FaceTime, Snapchat and live
stream

Talking on the phone is an old
timer's dream

Must we be in the same room,

I sent you five texts to consume

What makes me happy?

Counting my likes

Getting too old to just ride bikes

You tell me I'm never in view

Must you see me to have a clue?

I'm at your fingertips on that little screen
you hold

I'll come down now just for you and to
do as I am told

But you know I'm counting down when I
hear that beeping sound

To return to the social highway and the
virtual playground

REFLECTION

Here I go, here I go can't you see

Look at me, I'm VIP

Don't you see I run this place

Open your eyes, just look at my face

Every look and every glance

Snapping selfies when I get a chance

You don't like the way I flow?

Did you think this was your show?

As you walked in from afar,

Did you think you were the star?

It's all me, this light is mine

Every day's my time to shine

I'm on fire wherever I go,

Can't you see my everglow?

I can only be who I'm gonna be

Doesn't everyone want to be me?

As I trip in my own head

Living large 'til I go to bed

Am I still that girl you knew

From the playground who loved the color blue

I have more friends now than I know,

Who will always watch my show

They like me, they love me, they pump my head high

They follow my tracks as I glide in this social sky

When the network goes down and I freak out like a clown

Forced to remember who I was and what I'm about

Before my values you started to doubt

Digital detox is what I need, to correct this image I feed

I'm still me under this mask

Pretty soon I'll start to grasp

This can't last, I need to come back

Otherwise, you'll call me whack

CHANGING LANES

Racing down the highway, will he make it?

Three lanes to the left, I think he'll take it

Exit coming up ahead

Pay attention or you'll dread

The crash and burn that hurts your head

As it rolls and takes a dive

Hope you are still alive

Was it worth it, I say "no"

Take the next exit or away you'll go

From your chosen destination

A few more minutes to reach your location, you'll get there in due time

EYES ON THE ROAD

What happened to "keep your eyes
on the road"?

Is that text urgent enough to change
your mode?

From a conscious driver to jumping
lanes

Like a frolicking horse with an itchy
mane

Hands on the wheel, stay alert

Or my day you will divert

As I try to look behind

Wandering what is on your mind

You say you never saw me stop

But "how could you", I told the cop

It's so hard to watch you stare

At your phone without a care

Why can't you just put it down

And consider those around

We do care about our lives

As does everyone who drives

Take a moment to think this through

Can't they wait awhile for you?

Just pull over, if you can

Or we'll end up in a van

It's not good, I'll tell you that

It involves a rubber mat

And some sirens whirling 'round

As they lift us off the ground

I don't know what you had planned

But my day had some demand

We all have important places to go

So, let's get there safe, you know?

GOING BACK

Can you give me a lift?

As I walk down this road venturing into the unknown

Would you be my navigation and take me to the place I've always been

How'd I get here?

Am I lost?

Taking off blindly not considering the cost

With no fear to guide me back to those who care

Note to self – "don't do this again"

Better to stay home and find a friend

To discuss my situation

Instead of wandering to parts unknown
– like I'm grown

Help me find my way back. This was silly.

Can you give me a lift?

WHAT I KNOW

If you only knew

What I know about you

You would stop pretending to be
something you can't hide

Thinking we won't see inside

The pain, the fears, the heartbreak, the
tears

Life's too short to play this game

We both know it is quite lame

Let's be friends and drop the mask

And make joy our primary task

We don't know how long we're here

So, let's live our days with cheer

THE JOURNEY

How do I get from here to there

Can I risk it, do I dare

From dark to light and back to front

This is really not a stunt

I need to change my own
perspective

Trying to be a little more selective

I have to win, this is my chance

No time for jokes or a shaky stance

Focus solely on the next level

Procrastination is quite the devil

I've got big dreams that must come
true

Don't you understand why I do what I do?

Watch me rise and take things over

Just won't happen with a four-leaf clover

Work on it daily to master my craft

But today, all you do is laugh

You only see who I am now

Just you wait 'til I take a bow

Amidst the fame and wild applause

You'll understand it was for a cause

I've got one token for this ride

Making the best of it, He's my guide

FREE FLOW

(Epilogue)

If you've got something to say,

Say it.

Don't let anyone stop you from releasing what you've been given.

Hopefully you have found some inspiration in these pages.

Quiet your mind to turn on your creative faucet.

Looking forward to seeing how you will let it flow.

A.M.

www.ingramcontent.com/pod-product-compliance
Lightning Source LLC
LaVergne TN
LVHW010023070426
835508LV00001B/14